PROBLEMS

SOLVED

Public policies analyzed and solutions presented.

by Leon Czikowsky

Solutions Publishing

208 North Street

Harrisburg, PA. U.S.A. 17101-1124

INTRODUCTION

Many public policy books discuss the policy process. Few ever solve actual problems. This book is one that solves policy problems.

In my opinion.

Readers are free to agree or disagree. Yet I hope it enlightens them on policy questions. I hope it shows readers there are paths to solutions. Those who go into public policy should think how to resolve difficulties and do so in a manner that best helps people.

The solutions to many problems are simple. Yet the paths to these solutions often involve complicated routes. New ideas meet resistance from those comfortable with status quo responses. The greatest difficulties are often from those who have power and use their power to protect their interests over the public interest. Those with interests to protect are often very involved in policy making arenas concerning their interests.

We need more decision makers to represent the public in these interests.

ABOUT THE BOOK

These columns are from the website "Today's the Day-Harrisburg". They were professionally edited by Tara Lee Auchey. How she made sense from the author's ramblings shows what a miraculous editor she is.

This book will show how easy it could be to achieve world peace, save the environment, control climate change, improve education, and easily solve other complex public policy problems. In addition, many other problems such as drug and alcohol dependencies and unresolved mental health and intellectual disability issues can be prevented.

ABOUT THE AUTHOR

Gene Weingarten, a Washington Post columnist, once wrote of Leon Czikowsky, "You're a person without a soul. A damaged individual. It is as though you have been inexpertly lobotomized."

Fortunately, Gene Weingarten is a humor columnist.

The author is a former Research Specialist for the Human Services Committee of the Pennsylvania House of Representatives. Prior to that he held positions in legislative leadership and research offices. The door to his office had a sign reading "No One Important". His door was added to the Capitol tour,

Czikowsky served as a Legislative Liaison for the Drug and Alcohol Programs Department, worked for the U.S. Environmental Protection Agency, City Controller's office, and a local civic "good government" organization. Some believe his best work was delivering milk for Eugene Czikowsky, Jr. and Sons Dairy.

Czikowsky has a Masters of City and Regional Planning degree from the University of Pennsylvania, a Masters degree in Urban Studies from Southern Connecticut State, and a bachelors degree from the Wharton School of the University of Pennsylvania.

The author did not have a lobotomy..

COLUMNS

*

A One Way Ticket to Harrisburg's Haven

March 15, 2014

"I arrived in town on a one way ticket from Baltimore, and I just need a few dollars cash to eat."

"I'm from Newark. They gave me this one way ticket to Harrisburg and I need a few bucks for bus fare."

"I have this one way ticket I just used from Penn Station and I need some change so I can get settled."

As one who often rides the train and often walks along Sixth Street—a street strategically located on a straight line between the Amtrak Station and a homeless mission—I often encountered people begging for money. Their styles differ. Some are shy and seem afraid; others are quite aggressive. I even often find people asking for money inside the train station.

For years, I often wondered, what was it that makes beggars start their tales of woe with a story that they had recently arrived in town on a one way ticket?

What is the "street cred" that establishing one-self as a recent arrival makes one appear more sympathetic as a beggar? Are people more apt to give money if they think you are new to their community? Are people more prone to welcome new arrivals with cash? Eventually, I believe I learned why I often heard this story: Because it is true.

Harrisburg and Philadelphia have reputations for being generous with their services to homeless people. I fully support this. We should be proud that we reach out and help those in need. The problem is there are people who exploit our generosities. Part of this was Pennsylvania's own making.

There were unintended consequences in changes in Pennsylvania law. When people with drug and/or alcohol use problems were kicked off general welfare, what did people expect would happen? Did we expect people with dependencies would magically decide, since they've lost their benefits, they will now instantly decide to give up the substance(s) upon which they are dependent?

Many dependencies are found to alter brain functions. It often takes time and several attempts to overcome some dependencies. A drug dependency often requires a complex medical and often psychological recovery that differs for each person.

Many people who lost their benefits due to drug and/or alcohol issues were able to qualify for chronically needy benefits. These benefits were less monetarily yet held the likelihood of lasting longer. Since they were receiving less money, many people with dependencies could no longer afford housing. Still they were receiving money.

The result was the vast growth in the recovery home business.

The recovery home owners and operators recruit people with dependency issues who receive public assistance. They also may recruit and guide people towards qualifying for public assistance. A typical recovery home system is the residents pool their public assistance funds and give them to the recovery home operators. In return, the residents are to receive housing and recovery assistance.

Recovery homes are not regulated. There are good, bad, and ugly homes out there. Some are professionally staffed and provide excellent services to residents in overcoming their dependencies. The well-run ones often are recognized by people in the criminal justice system who steer troubled people dependent on drugs and/or alcohol towards these recovery homes.

Then there are bad ones that cram as many people as they can into the home and provide few or no actual services, Some are known to become places were drugs are used and sold.

Others are in-between. Some good programs involve counselors who are not professionals yet are people who have recovered themselves and counsel people how to similarly recover. These programs are probably only as good as the counselors, with some involved dedicated counselors and operators who have helped many people. Other homes have staffers who lack the knowledge to properly counsel others.

Because these homes are not regulated, there is uncertainty as to how many there are. The Public Welfare Department (DPW) supposedly was making an attempt to discover this.

They can note when a large number of assistance checks go to the same address. There were also reports of homes in Scranton and elsewhere with horrific conditions that may have prodded them into actions. It is believed DPW originally started looking at this for welfare fraud purposes and instead are finding a large number of recovery homes. It is not yet clear how much effort is being put into this nor what their plans are. Yet perhaps DPW will someday determine how many recover homes there are. A Temple University researcher a few years ago estimated there were 400 to 500 in Philadelphia. I have seen no estimates for how many are in Harrisburg.

Another problem is, since Pennsylvania is now known as the state with lots of recovery homes, others have taken advantage.

There are programs in Baltimore and New Jersey that have admitted that one of the ways they handle their problems with homeless people with drug and/or alcohol dependencies is to give them a one way ticket to Philadelphia or Harrisburg along with the name of a homeless shelter.

Some report that New York City—especially during their "clean up the city" days of a former mayor—sent homeless people to Pennsylvania. The Temple University researcher found evidence that groups in Puerto Rico were giving people one way air flights to Pennsylvania. Philadelphia officials once sought actions against New Jersey officials for sending too many New Jersey homeless to Philadelphia,

These new arrivals are often prime targets for recovery home recruitment, once they qualify for public assistance. (I presume if one could afford to pay to enter a home, such a person would not be rejected. I once asked some experts if this happens and I was greeted with a blank stare and a statement that "no one pays their own money to enter one of these homes." While I gather few would pay to live with recent homeless people, it seems apparent the recovery programs are not well regarded by experts.) Recruiters literally search the streets and attend AA and similar group meetings looking for potential residents.

So, we may congratulate ourselves on being more caring about the homeless than many of our neighbors. In my opinion, we now need to act to see that people in these recovery homes are getting proper shelter and treatment. The shelter part may be easier to inspect. The treatment part is more difficult to assess, as those with lower success rates may actually have more difficult cases.

There are some ways to legally take actions against badly run recovery homes. Inspections could determine if the homes are livable. Further, if a recovery home has become a nuisance in terms of repeated drug dealing violations and the owner and operator appear unable to prevent the home from being a repeat drug dealing offender, chances are good that is a hazardous residence that should be closed. Some local communities have nuisance ordinances that would accomplish this.

These homes should be regulated, in my opinion. There should at the very least be minimal standards that protect the residents. The problem is the recovery home owners do not want to be regulated. Some people have been able to make themselves wealthy by owning recovery homes. Many of the recovery homes actively work the political system to prevent attempts at regulating them. Some recovery homes have created, in the name of providing them treatment assistance, programs getting residents to volunteer in political campaigns and to lobby elected officials against creating regulations. If one wants an example of wealthy people getting poor people to actively work to keep the wealthy people rich, this is a good one.

A cycle exists. Because we provide services to a greater proportion of the homeless and people in need compared to other nearby states, more homeless and people in need come, or are sent, to our state. So, when one makes the observation that there seem to be more homeless and people in need on our streets or train stations than we see in other cities, that may be an accurate statement.

Sadly, we do not have enough resources to provide proper services to all who need them. Therein lies the real

tragedy.**

****

Sexual Assault Is Nothing to Joke About

April 5, 2014

Humor is the brain processing incongruent thoughts and realizing they don't fit together. Why the human body responds with laughter, I do not know. It is more practical than responding with hiccups

.

Maybe humans used to respond by either laughing or striking out violently against the person who made the non-compatible statements, and over time those who laughed out-survived those who attacked.

Harrisburg has a Comedy Club. I have been to this club several times.

Jokes have been told at this club. Which is sort of the point. People joke about relationships, current events, celebrities, rape, etc.

Except, rape jokes are not funny.

The reason they are not funny is it's not incompatible ideas that could never happen. Some surveys have found approximately one sixth of the females in the audience, on average, have been sexually assaulted. It is not funny to them. It can bring back traumatic memories.

Still the debate about rape jokes rages within the comedic world. I have read some humorists argue that all jokes are protected by freedom of speech. It is fair to joke about anything.

I have read others describe there are some rape jokes that are alright. They argue there is a critical difference between making the rape victim the brunt of the joke or making the attacker the joke's target. Perhaps making fun of the system that makes reporting and prosecuting rape is fine

.

Some argue that any rape joke is wrong. It upsets too many people who had to live through or live with someone who was raped.

One key to any performance is you have to appeal to the audience that is paying money to watch and listen the show. If there is no audience, there is no show.

I believe that one has to be sensitive to the reality that a number of people, men and women, have been raped or faced an attempted assault. They did not pay to be needlessly emotionally hurt by a performance with others around them laughing at the cause of their pains.

This discussion explodes in magnitude when one considers data from the Institutional Betrayal Questionnaire that was completed by 345 college females. This found that almost half of those surveyed had been sexually assaulted.

Almost half is much higher than one sixth. One half of young females is dramatically higher than one sixth over lifetimes.

Is this Institutional Betrayal Questionnaire an outlier whose results are not consistent with other studies? Or is this telling us something important?

Perhaps young people are experiencing more attacks. Perhaps young people are more aware and more willing to step forward and identify attacks that people older than them used to ignore.

Over one third of the assaults reported by these college students were institutional assaults. This mean they were forced against their will to have sex with someone who was their boss, teacher, religious figure, judicial system officer, military commander, etc.

Perhaps in the past we chose to be blind to such assaults. We are now more aware and open about this. We have seen locally where several teachers, male and female, have been arrested for seducing students. We have witnessed the sex scandals at universities and places of worship.

Are these recent arrests just a few among many? This also leads to the next discussion: If there are so many attacks, how are so many attackers getting away with it?

Jennifer Freyd, a former social issues activist in Pennsylvania, left our state and now teaches Psychology at the University of Oregon. She was involved in this Institutional

Betray Questionnaire and has written about how we tend to be blind to various kinds of assaults and betrayal.

We are blind to the betrayal of assault for numerous reasons. The brain protects itself from trauma by subsiding the disturbing memory. When the perpetrator is someone one respects or has some dependency upon—such as an employer or partner—one often puts more importance on the positive aspects of continuing the relationship than one puts on the negative, abusive points.

Harrisburg has been relatively silent. According to the FBI's Uniform Crime Report, for the most recent year where data has been released, 2010, there were no reports of forcible rape in Harrisburg reported to law enforcement that year.

Yet assaults happen. We may turn away when it is an institutional assault. When a boss, teacher, or religious figure uses power over another, we pretend it is not an assault. We may consider it consensual or, turned back before an assault occurs, pretend it didn't happen.

We need to learn to recognize abuse and betrayals and to speak up. There are dangers to doing this. People often disbelieve accusers. Because the mind subjugates traumatic experiences, accusers may not recall all the facts. Complacency and failure to speak before is after turned around and claimed to have been consent.

Institutional assaults can be very destructive, both to the individual assaulted and to the institution. It destroys the truth we have in the institution, both from the assaulted and from those aware or suspicious it happened. In working in Harrisburg, I've heard of instances where a boss promoted an employee for sex. That creates an extremely difficult work environment for all involved.

I often joke about the time I was approached about providing a character witness for someone. I replied, "He was very kind employer to both his mistresses." For some reason, I was not called to testify.

If abuse is increasing, or even if we are recognizing it more, there are some trends we need to reverse We need more school counselors who are trained in handling abuse cases.If these problems are so prevalently reported by college students, many of their problems happened before college. By catching problems earlier in life, so many longer terms problems can be prevented and minimized.

It is hard to advocate for increased counseling in a time when our schools are barely able to provide basic educational programs. We need to join in making state government aware that counselors are necessary. They also need to realize this will save them money down the road as abused children as more apt to be causes of expensive future social services.

We also need to listen. It is true that not every accusation is true. Yet we need to stop hiding from these problems. By letting people know that if.they voice the knowledge of their betrays, there are people who will listen and not judge.

It is also important that abusers and potential abusers hear these messages. They need to realize these actions and wrong. They must know that people will speak out if they abuse.

We as a society need to do all this. We have been blind to betrayals on many levels. We need to speak out, listen, and act against many types of abuses. Many have looked the other way when horrific crimes such as genocide occurred. Many do not get involved when they see local corruption. We need to learn to speak out more.

It is good people are talking about this. When it is pointed out how many famous comedians in the past told rape jokes, we must remember that was back in a time when people did not talk about this. So it was seldom discussed, and thus struck people as incongruent thoughts back then to talk about it.

Yet, the fact we are talking about it is raising awareness of rape and assaults to new levels. We are realizing that assaults, even if not successfully completed or become consensual, are especially wrong when those with power of someone else abuses that power. That people are opening up about.

This is serious. It is not a joke.

****

Regionalization Brings It Together

May 3, 2014

The news that Dauphin County police departments are researching creating a regionalized police force is good news. Regionalization, overall, is a good thing.

One force policing a larger area should be an improvement. Crime data and response plans would be more centralized. This should be more effective stopping and catching criminals.

The feeling of working together within the region often makes a critical difference. By comparison, people engaging in jurisdictional fights in support of their agency over a neighboring agency is counterproductive.

Moving to regionalization often improves administrative functions. Instead of management decisions made in each local force, decisions which may not well work or even conflict with another force, decisions are made considering what is best overall. Regionalization should create more effective operations.

Regionalization should save money. Instead of wasting money purchasing the same materials for each of several local police force, with regionalization, duplicate purchases can be eliminated. No longer will each police force require its own vehicle fleet, equipment, etc. Economies of scales for goods and services can lower overall costs. The use of police services and equipment can be both better coordinated and accomplished at reduced expenses.

Pennsylvania has an amazing number of localities. 48 states have fewer numbers of towns and cities. Each Pennsylvania locality has its own local government. These governments do not provide all local public services.

There are separate schools districts and authorities that do not share the same geographic boundaries as local governments. Regionalization has worked well throughout the country. Pennsylvania, with its strong local government history and culture, has been slow to adapt to the benefits of regionalization. It especially is useful to move towards regionalization in areas involving public safety.

The large number of authorities in Pennsylvania creates a special concern. Authorities are able to take on large amounts of debt and sometimes the residents are left holding large authority debt from improper economic forecasting or mismanagement. This is especially frustrating to citizens as they have less contact with agency officials than elected officials.

Critical issues emerge emerge when paying large authority debts. This makes it more difficult for a local government to continue properly supporting its local police force. Thus regionalization should be considered for a number of public services including police.

A caution to note is that regionalized police should always operate on what is best for the public safety. The services should not be influenced by "squeaky wheel" wealthier areas with less crime who may insist on receiving more than their fair share of services. This reduces the ability to address crime where it exists more. Communities with less political influence should not be ignored and given fewer services than they require. A frequent objection to regionalization is that there will be job losses. Those with positions are often those who most strongly fight changes to their status quo. If they see they will keep their position, their opposition often reduces or disappear.

In my opinion, I do not wish to see people's livelihoods destroyed by regionalization, especially when many have undergone special training to obtain their jobs. There is often a benefit to institutional knowledge, especially when creating a new system. I believe it improves morale and is kinder if there are no job losses. If there are economies of scale that are achieved by less staffing, I would encourage that these be achieved by attrition.

A regional police force may better coordinate with other county services. For example, many victimless crimes are of drug use. People with dependences on drugs and or alcohol are often better served in counseling than in jail. Jail cells are usually places where people with dependences make contacts with other criminals, Convicts often teach newly imprisoned how to become better criminals and how to further their drug use. County social services and drug agencies should find it easier to offer services with one regional police department. It is more troublesome dealing wit several different police entities when determining with them sentencing alternatives.

A regional police force may better coordinate activities with other law enforcement agencies, such as the State Police, Federal Bureau of Investigations, and other similar agencies. It should be easier to communicate and act in cooperation with other agencies when they may deal with one agency for the area instead of multiple agencies.

Regionalization allows more efficient streamlining of operations. It better allows for cooperation with others. It ends bitter divisiveness between local authorities. Plans and actions can better be made for more people in a larger area. Duplication of purchases and personnel functions saves money and further improve functions.

If local leaders can put aside their local biases and look at the overall good, regionalization can be created. Sometimes it is imposed by a county or state government authority and may be met with local resistance.

There have been times when attempts at regionalization fail because they are never given the chance as its enemies work to make it fail. Regional leaders must be given the ability to succeed.

A regional police force, if given the chance, can be created and should be allowed to show it may work.

****

May 21, 2012

A Computer Glitch and A City Council Candidate Application Is Lost

A benefit with this site, "today's the day Harrisburg", is it often has interesting links to click. A few weeks ago, it included a link to become an applicant for the Harrisburg City Council vacancy.

I had no expectation that if I clicked that link, I would ever be selected for the vacancy. I understand politics enough to know that someone with connections to a majority of Council members will be selected. In fact, I would be more surprised if the selection was not one derived from politics. One expects politicians to be highly political.

With one easy click, one could be a candidate. I thought, why not? Not only would I have the opportunity, as a commentator, to force Council members to read my views (of course, I expect that all Council members read my contributions here, right? right?) yet I would be able to get a view of the selection process from the viewpoint of an applicant. I figured that ought to be worthwhile writing about.

Indeed, I do have some observations that are worth writing about. It was not at all what I ever expected.

As the process moved along and I heard nothing after I submitted my application, I figured Council realized it would be a waste of both of our times to interview me. That did not bother me. I never expected to be considered.

Then one day, I returned at 6 pm to have a phone message left at 4:30 pm (yes, I still have an old fashioned telephone) telling me my application had been lost. Then found.

And while Council had already narrowed the process to two finalists, I was invited to speak for two minute s before Council at 5:30. Which was then a half hour past. I would have been happier had I never received this call.

How does one "lose" an application, which obviously had not been lost if it had been "found" at the last moment?

I understand there was a glitch with a city computer. I understand that. Glitches are a part of what we have to put up with for the convenience of computers.Overall, though, computers are far less likely to lose something than the old system of manual filing.

I have no reason to believe my "lost" then "found" application was anything deliberate. Misplacing it should not have made any difference on the final outcome. Yet it does indicate a need for more oversight over public sector computers and information technology departments.

Although, if I later learn other applications were lost, then I would very, very concerned. [Editor's Note: There were four applications affected by "computer glitches." Two because of a firewall issue, two because they were located after-the-fact in "spam"]

We need to know when computers are not working properly. Computer errors on more serious things—from tax records to criminal warrants—could significantly and needlessly disrupt or harm lives. If there are computer maintenance issues or programming errors, they need to be caught earlier rather than later.

If there is an employee abusing the system, oversight needs to promptly catch this. The most powerful person in city government may not, at times, be the Mayor. It can be the person in charge of the city's information technology.

San Francisco learned this lesson the hard way. Their head of their information technology systems, for a few days, refused to give anyone the password to turn on the city government's computers. Many city departments essentially stopped functioning during that period.

No city should ever allow itself to be held hostage by its own information technology office.

Nor should any government allows itself to shut down because it can't turn on its computers, for whatever reason.

A problem is elected officials usually are not information technology specialists. They do not have the ability to tell if information technology expenses and procedures are legitimate . Elected officials usually lack the knowledge to know if an information technology office is being managed properly.

Elected government administrators should not have to accept the word of information technology managers as to how their offices should be run and at what cost. This is important as information technology offices are achieving greater shares of city budgets.

The solution is easy. Government needs to hire computer savvy experts to oversee information technology departments. These experts need to audit information technology practices, codes, and hardware. They need to eliminate waste and duplication. They must determine if things are operating efficient and effectively. They have to check that upgrades occur as they should.

Those auditing information technology need to guarantee what they oversee works fine. If code is not written correctly, or is written so complexly that only the author can understand it, it is of no use to co-workers or future employees. If operating systems are designed improperly, future employees may discover they are unable to continue past work. There have been information technology employees who have secured their positions by making themselves the only people who know how to operate things.

So much responsibility should not be held in the hands of a few people who can then imperil government. Left unchecked, they can create positions where only they know how to do their jobs. They can then hide from the public what they do and how they do it.

This can create serious problems. It could give them undue weight in determining their own budgets and demanding funds they don't really need. If no one else understands their true budget needs, taxpayers can end up paying needless expenses, Difficulties can emerge if employees with such proprietary knowledge are away during emergencies. A new employee can't continue past work if the work can only be understood by the former employee.

The actions can destroy an office. It's a dereliction of the duty of elected officials to hand over so much authority to people who can then abuse it. They must allow for oversight.

Our state government has already realized how much this can cost. The Labor and Industry Department spent over a hundred million dollars on computer operations that do not work. How does any project go that far along without anyone realizing it was on the wrong path? There is a strong need for knowledgable people checking that things are not going astray. The cost savings in such oversight can be enormous.

Even physicians recommend patients obtain a second opinion on their health concerns. Few people know enough about surgery or writing computer code to determine, on their own, what procedures are best in any given situation.

Clearly, we need second opinions on our city's public sector information technology systems. This time it was a citizen's application lost. However, the financial costs of not having oversight can be enormous.

We must guarantee we have a government that works for us, not one that shuts down on us due to some glitch.

****

Harrisburg's City Government's Financial Crisis

June 24, 2014

If there are lessons to be learned from studying how other cities emerged from the brink—or reality, of being bankrupt—one lesson stands out: No city ever solved its financial crisis on its own.

Some cities that turned around their economic misfortunes did so by merging services with their suburbs or even incorporating suburbs with their stronger tax bases into city boundaries.

Others did so with assistance from state and/or Federal governments. In rare cases the city government was able to take actions to save itself, yet it did so by attracting a major private employer or investor whose resources pulled it to solvency.

Harrisburg city government is functionally bankrupt, in that it cannot pay all that it owes. However, it is not legally allowed to be bankrupt. The laws protect the bond holders from bankruptcy action. Harrisburg appears to be drifting into an uncertain long term future while hoping that a way to survive will be found.

There are short term solutions. It is ironic, though, that items that produce long term revenues, such as parking and even the incinerator, which began showing signs of being able to be operated profitably, are traded for short term revenues. In the long run, these revenues to Harrisburg will likely be reduced.

There are also serious concerns that the new higher parking rates may drive customers and even residents away from Harrisburg. This is the opposite of what is needed for a city's economy to grow.

New York City was saved from near bankruptcy in the 1970s to 1980s primarily due to assistance from the state and Federal governments (see The Year the Big Apple Went Bust, a book by Fred Feretti). Congress and President Gerald Ford approved loaning New York City $2.4 billion. The Ford Administration, despite the famous misquote that

President Ford supposedly told New York City to "drop dead,", provided New York City with critically needed loans. The Carter Administration continued this assistance.

New York's Governor and the state legislature advanced New York City $400 million. The Governor personally helped convince bankers and union pension funds to invest in bonds that balanced the city's budget (see The Man Who Saved New York by Seymour Lachman)

.

As in 1933 when New York City also faced bankruptcy, a state government assistance agency was created. This agency purchased New York City's short term debt which helped save the city government financially.

Others cities were saved from the path of financial ruin by large infusions of Federal government funds. These include Philadelphia and Boston. It should be to noted that many of these Federal government programs no longer exist. Thus, this option is extremely limited.

Cities such as Indianapolis and Denver survived financially by annexing their suburbs. That is not an option as Pennsylvania law prohibits annexations and makes merges very difficult. Of course, the state law could be changed.

At this time, there are few leading the way for this state law change. Such a proposal would likely be resisted by suburbs who wish to keep their wealthier tax bases within their own communities. Passage of a law allowing annexation or easing the way for merges will probably require a realization from suburbanites that their communities' financial futures are directly linked to the futures of their cities' finances. Today, such recognition does not appear to be widespread.

Harrisburg supplies the region with much of the region's arts, museums, professional athletics, etc. It is where major employers such as state government, hospitals, and numerous businesses are. The suburbs resulted from government investments in highway systems that allowed more affluent urban residents to flee urban areas and create suburban communities. The suburbs have fewer per capita social needs and operating costs compared to cities The social needs and costs of cities increased. It is time for urbanites and suburbanites to work together on regional economic planning and actions.

Another possible change in the law could allow Harrisburg to declare bankruptcy. While this is not what bond holders want to hear, Harrisburg needs to become a city that grows economically. If constantly paying for debt halts improving the city, it may be better that the city defaults.

In an historic analogy, both France and Great Britain had large debts in the mid-18th century. France defaulted on two thirds of its debt in 1797. Free from this debt, France engaged in an era of more rapid economic development.

Great Britain, on the other hand, let its debt grow to twice its Gross Domestic Product. It took a century for Great Britain to pay that debt. This drained its ability to grow its economy. Paying the debt benefited the wealthy British bond holders. This contributed towards national wealth inequities that helped slow economic growth even more. Money in the hands of the middle class and poor is spent more quickly and increases demand leading to the creation of more goods (see Capital in the Twenty-first Century by Thomas Piketty)

Once a city averts a financial crisis, it then needs to improve its economic situation. Cities do this by improving their infrastructures and creating quality mass transit systems. This attracts new investors and residents, according to a study at The Brookings Institution.

It seems highly questionable that Harrisburg has the resources within its tax base to accomplish what is needed to economically improve itself. The amount of tax free property within Harrisburg and the relative lower incomes that Harrisburg residents have compared to other municipalities makes it difficult to raise the required revenues.

The relative advanced age of the Harrisburg's infrastructure makes repairing it an expensive item. Sadly, the lack of a good infrastructure can prevent growth and even contribute to an exodus from the city. Also, since Harrisburg is the capital city, a declining infrastructure makes it more difficult for state government to operate.

Some cities have had an outside venture help save its city government. Cleveland saw tourism help its economy when the Rock and Roll Hall of Fame Museum, three new sports stadiums, and a Science Center located there.

Other cities have had their business, community, and government leaders work together to find ways to attract new investors. Boston, Seattle, and New York have taken different paths to attract entrepreneurs, engineering ventures, residential investors, etc.

There is no one set plan that guarantees urban economic growth. Each city found its own process that helped its own city. Yet each city did plan and act. Again, it was important that certain things were in place to attract this growth, such as a strong infrastructure, good schools, solid mass transit options.

Perhaps Harrisburg will develop a strategy that will attract a an outside financial savior.

Or maybe the Federal and/or state government will create new programs that will help pull Harrisburg out of its economic troubles and push it towards economic growth.

Or perhaps the suburban residents will realize that the life of Harrisburg determines their continued economic vitality.

Or will the state government leaders realize they rely upon Harrisburg for their very functioning? While state government makes payments in lieu of taxes, those payments are much less than what would be paid if the properties required city taxes payments.

If the state government and region continues to deny the stark reality of Harrisburg's fiscal situation, the alternative may be that the Commonwealth eventually finds itself forced to accept Harrisburg as its financial ward. It would be less expensive, as well as allowing Harrisburg residents to better determine their own policies, if Harrisburg is allowed to continue operating on its own with the state government's help.

There are options but the fact is that Harrisburg requires help. Let's see who answers its call.

****

What If the City of Harrisburg Transformed Itself With Algae?

August 1, 2014

Imagine if there were a new, emerging industry that could locate in Harrisburg that would solve all of its financial problems.

It's an industry that could solve our energy problems. In addition, it could change our international business situation by ending our reliance on foreign oil at the same time as helping solve the climate change problem.

One word—algae.

Algae produces more fuel than does any other known fuel producing process. It is also the least expensive.

One acre of algae can produce 5,000 gallons of fuel. The closest any competing fuel source can accomplish is palm oil. One acre of palm oil produces 800 gallons of fuel. A great convenience of algae is that it can grow just about anywhere. It can grow in dirty water. It would not need to be located any existing ground used for croplands.

Algae does not have to use current cropland to grow. Our food supply would not have to be reduced in order to grow algae.

Just about the least efficient means to obtain fuel is to drill in the ground for it. That is also the most expensive way to get fuel.

The least expensive manner of creating fuel is to convert algae into fuel. Unlike cane sugar (used in Brazil and other countries) and corn (used in ethanol), which can grow once or twice a year, algae grows by itself, year round. It does not take much to grow algae. Ask anyone who ever owned a pool.

Shell Oil was researching using algae as fuel. Raytheon was developing algae for fuel. In fact, it was successfully used for flying military jets.

Then something unusual (or usual, depending upon your level of political cynicism) happened. Congress cut funding for research for studying converting algae into fuel. Although, I have to give my respects to the military. Their researchers keep going forward. The Navy has developed a way to use sea water for fuel. See United States Naval Research Laboratory.

No matter the naysayers, fact is we appear to be on the verge of developing algae or some inexpensive alternative for vehicle fuel. If planes can fly with algae as fuel as has been proven, surely we can figure out how to use it for cars.

We will then have the least expensive means of producing vehicle fuel that is also the most productive way to obtain the most fuel.

However, for some reason, we are currently set on using the most expensive process that yields the least amount of fuel.

Whoever first develops algae as fuel for "everyday living," wins an economic game. The potential payback could be enormous.

State Rep. David Kessler is a visionary who saw Pennsylvania as the place where this could be achieved. He served two terms yet was defeated in 2010 for reelection to a third term.

It is Pennsylvania's heritage to find new fuel sources. The oil industry began here. Why not the next generation of fuel?

Some believe one of our major college research facilities, at perhaps Penn State or Temple University, could be the ones that find the final, missing pieces.

Yet here's the significant, and, yes, perhaps radical question—Why not Harrisburg? There is great potential and talent at Harrisburg University. There are sharp minds among its students and faculty who could be just the ones able to think through the roadblocks and develop algae for fuel.

Let's imagine again.

Imagine if Harrisburg became the center for algae and other alternative energy research and development. We have the affordable land and buildings. We are near an airport with a long runway to accommodate foreign visitors.

Now for the kicker: Growing an abundance of algae reduces climate change problems. Sixty percent of our oxygen is produced by algae. Algae, which is one half of one percent of our planet's plant biomass, produces a lot of oxygen. Algae absorbs carbon dioxide. Carbon dioxide is a major cause of climate change. Growing a lot more algae should reduce carbon dioxide and improve our climate (If you are a recent contestant for the Republican nomination for President, you may wish to disregard this paragraph).

It would be great to see Harrisburg academicians, business leaders, and community members get together and explore this. Obviously, this is a long shot. Yet the initial steps are not difficult. If this takes off, the opportunities are ripe with possibility.

Many cities have grown from one new idea. New York City is current expanding business investment by providing large city government investments in engineering research and development. New engineering firms are locating around the New York City colleges that have expanded their engineering schools.

Algae research and development, in my non-expert analysis, should not be that difficult to complete. A little investment in this field could go a long way.

Quite frankly, though, the economic development spark for Harrisburg does not have to be algae.

This is just a recommendation of the type of breakthrough activity that can turn a city's economy around. Perhaps there is a better fit for Harrisburg. In the developing fields of other emerging fields, such as nanotechnologies, perhaps our residents may find a better fit for a new economic entrant that will improve our local economy.

We should begin the search and see what we may create and attract.

Wouldn't it be great if that next innovative thing happened in Harrisburg?

****

Harrisburg Tourism

September 21, 2014

A good method for local officials to better understand tourists is to try to view their locality as tourists find the area.

Recently, Harrisburg hosted a conference of a group to which I belonged. Since I had traveled to various cities for this organization, I already had experienced many of the problems tourists face with unfamiliar surroundings.

While our guests were in the city, I wondered how they fared visiting Harrisburg. So I asked them. Keeping in mind what our visitors stated, I then attempted to view Harrisburg as a tourist might.

I concluded the main physical attractions (not counting periodic attractions such as festivals and sports games) in Harrisburg are the Civil War Museum (while technically outside the city, it is owned by the city government), the State Capitol, the Whitaker Center, the Fire Museum, and the John Harris Museum.

Here are some observation based on my time thinking about being a tourist in the City of Harrisburg:

A striking discovery is many residents do not know how to tell a tourist how to get to some of these places. Hotel, restaurant, and services staff often do not know how to give directions to these spots of interest, either.

More effort should be made to increase residents' awareness of these attraction—well-placed brochures, mailers, & billboards. Further, finding ways to attract local residents to these attractions (i.e. discounts or special features according to attendees' zip codes) would help.

If people do not wish to drive to any of these locations and wish to use mass transit, even fewer local residents could tell a tourist how to do so. For the John Harris Museum, the correct answer is you can't get there by bus. Fortunately, the John Harris Museum, the State Capitol, and the Whitaker Center are walkable from the Downtown hotels, but unfortunately that's not true of all of the city's worthwhile sights.

For example, when talking about the Civil War Museum and Fire Museum, there is nothing on the bus schedules which mention even which bus lines go near these museums. There is no advertising on the maps that layout museum stops. There are no directions about the shorts walks to reach these museums.

The bus system is designed for commuters. The schedules and printed bus schedules are meant for commuter use. There is nothing wrong with this, as the bus officials are meeting their customer needs. Yet, if we wish to get tourists to feel comfortable using our bus system, some easily achievable changes could assist.

The printed bus schedules could include more landmarks, including what commercial, entertainment, and museums are located along and near the bus routes. The front page of the bus schedules, which list bus destinations, should include listing the museums. At present, the schedules do not mention them.

It is also advisable the bus schedules use a bolder and larger font. One of the complaints I received from people with vision difficulties who wanted to explore the area by bus is the schedules were difficult to read. It would help if the schedules were easier to read.

It would be helpful to tourists, new residents, and casual bus riders who may not be familiar with the bus system if bus stops would include the bus number(s) at the bus stops. This would especially be useful in the Downtown areas where several buses stop at different nearby locations. It helps ridership if people are standing at the correct stop. Speaking of numbers, the bus numbers should appear on the back of the buses as well as on the front.

It is good to see plans to place the Downtown bus originations closer to the train station. It is also good to see that Amtrak is planning a stop close to the airport. It helps tourists if transportation modes transfers are easier to reach. At present, transferring from one mass transit mode to another may be confusing as the transfer areas are uncommonly further distances from each other.

Lastly, an issue that needs consideration is the current use of the bus transfer area as outdoor homeless shelters. The city should offer those who choose to be outdoors and homeless better accommodations. In speaking with visitors, especially those staying at the Downtown Crowne Plaza, the presence of the homeless and pan handlers at the Market Square bus area is a deterrent to visitors going past that area. They thus are deterred from walking to the Downtown restaurants and other attractions.

The Capitol building is an integral part of Harrisburg tourism. The Pennsylvania Capitol is the largest Capitol building in the nation. According to Smithsonian magazine, it is the "most ornate" of the Capitol buildings. It should be a key tourist destination.

A problem many tourists note is the State Capitol has a small gift shop. Having been to several State Capitols, I can confirm this. I find it hard to imagine that the largest Capitol in the country is unable to find enough room to accommodate the desires of tourists to spend money.

Even more ironic is some of the better quality gifts that the Pennsylvania Capitol has to offer are sold from an office on the Capitol's top floor. There are few directional signs within the building guiding tourists to this shop. These items should be sold in a shop experiencing higher tourist traffic.

We have an excellent Fire Museum. I have been to several fire museums in other cities, and ours stands out amongst the best. What it lacks is attendees. The Fire Museum should be part of an organized attempt to get people to not only come to Harrisburg, yet to have seeing this museum as among their reasons in which to increase their stay.

I was surprised at the recent suggestions by some that the Civil War Museum be closed. On the contrary, Harrisburg stands to benefit from the tourism this museum attracts. It should be used to entice more visitors. It was always a logical idea to attempt to attract the many tourists who visit two of the busiest Pennsylvania attractions, namely Gettysburg and Hersheypark. Harrisburg is between these two.

Having the best Civil War Museum should especially entice the Gettysburg tourists wishing to learn more about the Civil War. The Civil War Museum is critical for attracting these tourist dollars. We should be encouraging local hotels to offer free or low cost shuttles to Civil War Museum, which would also help attract tourists to book at these hotels.

As much as this next statements may attract some angry resentments, the dead projects of creating more museums would have been steps in the right direction. There are good arguments over which types of museums would have been best. Certainly the manner in which they were handled warranted criticism. Ultimately, though, the issue of creating more museums should be revisited.

A Wild West Museum could have attracted visitors to the area who are not able to travel to the Western U.S. to see their wild west museums. (Indeed, there really aren't that many such museums out west, anyway.) An assortment of museums, such as an African American Museum and a sports museum would draw a mixture of tourists. There should have been public debate over what that mix of museums should be. Those ideas were decent ones. Such ideas should be rekindled, and done so in open public discussion with the museums created with public oversight.

An issue that several tourists complain about is the airport taxi service. One company has a monopoly over picking up passengers. It was reported in the Patriot News that this would be done to punish a competitor who overcharged. Yet experiences show that rides from the airport into Harrisburg are often about twice what is charged for rides from Harrisburg to the airport from all taxi services. This makes one wonder if overcharging is now institutionalized.

Further, it is frustrating for airport arrivers to discover there are no taxis outside. One driver told me the company with the airport monopoly also has a county contract and that while he was coming to pick up a passenger, the county contract called and the county receives priority over airport passengers.

A representative from a competing cab company stated his driver could pick up a passenger at the airport but the driver would have to pay a surcharge which meant the driver would lose money taking a passenger from the airport into Harrisburg. Whatever the facts are, the airport's taxi service needs to improve. The reputation of Harrisburg as a tourist destination depends upon it.

Innovation

The city needs innovative ideas in attracting tourists. A city in Vietnam decorated its bridge to look like a dragon which brings people to see the bridge. The Colorado State Capitol has a winter lights display that pulls in lots of cars driving by. We could decorate our pedestrian bridge. Our Capitol or City Hall could have a night lights show. There could be lots of other ideas. There could be a competition on what could be done— indeed, several good projects could be done— and some of the funds designated for the arts could be used to invest in something innovative where the arts could attract tourists.

Harrisburg is in a good location between major tourist attractions, connected to several highways, is a rail terminating station, and has an international airport. With a few steps in the right direction, it can find financial success attracting tourists.

****

Solving Harrisburg's School Problems

October 17, 2014

The solutions to Harrisburg's education crisis are simple.

Often we look at complex problems and analyze the multiple challenges the problems present and believe there is only a complex solution to a complicated problem.

That is not necessarily true

.

A main problem is too many Harrisburg students are leaving high school without the proper knowledge required to enter college or without adequate preparation for employment. This is because schools often pass along failing students until they either reach the age to drop out of school or they graduate without providing them with the necessary education.

The solution can be achieved by administrative changes.
Schools should schedule their basic courses, such as English, Mathematics, and Sciences at the same time for each grade. Each student attends the grade level of each course that is appropriate for each student's level of achievement. No student is promoted to the next level until proficiency is achieved at the level in which the student is currently enrolled.

Most people excel in a subject and often find another subject more challenging. This system recognizes that. Students who are exceptionally bright in a subject should be promoted more quickly. Holding them back often makes them bored. They often perform worse in a subject where they already understand the material. They may become bored, pay less attention, fail to apply themselves. and thus underachieve.

The key to this system is to not promote students in each subject level before they are ready for the next level. If they cannot achieve at a lower level, they are bound to fail at a higher level. Promoting students to levels that are beyond their grasp virtually guarantees they will never catch up. Yet this is what often happens. When a student is promoted to the next grade for all classes yet is deficient in a specific area, that deficiency generally become greater in higher grades.

Students should be assigned to their age appropriate home rooms. This lessens the stigma students face when they are failed a grade. Everyone of the same age is in their age appropriate grade level home room. For example, there might be well be a third grader, in third grade home room, who is in second grade English, third grade Science, and fourth grade Mathematics.

There could be high achievers in specific courses who are several levels ahead. There could be students troubled with some areas who will need extra time. The grade level assignments should be what is appropriate for that student.

Every student is different.

In summary, what needs to happen is no student only reaches the next level in a subject before the student is ready for that level.

There are other ways to improve Harrisburg schools that are simple to implement yet more difficult to achieve. The schools need better funding, and those funds need to be spent on improving education. Teacher salaries should be increased. It is hard to attract the best teachers to the schools with the lowest salaries. It is especially hard to encourage our best college students to become teachers when other professions pay much better.

It is interesting to learn the views of others (including policy makers) who live in school districts with higher student achievements whose schools receive more per funds per student. Some of them, incorrectly in my opinion, argue that the school districts receiving less funds per student who have lower student achievement levels do not deserve to have more funds "wasted" on them. Education seems to be just about the only issue where people look at the problems, see where the difficulties are, and then believe the problems will miraculously improve themselves by neglecting them.

It is true that many Harrisburg students may face more social problems than do many suburban students. Teachers and school administrators alone cannot resolve all these social problems. Yet this should tell us that those with more social problems require more assistance, not less. These are the schools that need more counselors, tutors, and after school programs to further encourage student achievements. If these things do not exist, the alternatives for many students are being on the streets or being home alone.

We need to identify students with learning or social problems and provide them assistance to overcome their troubles. If we do not reach out and help troubled students while they are young, these social problems are very apt to become more costly societal problems in terms of underemployment, crime, etc.

A few decades ago, courts across the nation ruled that the state school funding inequities between richer and poorer school districts were illegal. Pennsylvania found itself on the cutting edge as the courts ruled Pennsylvania's inequities did not meet the criteria that the courts had found illegal. Since then, the inequities in school funding in Pennsylvania appear to have increased.

There is a current court case that once again is raising the funding inequities in Pennsylvania. It will not surprise me if the courts find Pennsylvania has slid into the realm of illegal inequities. While it may take the actions of courts rather than Pennsylvania citizens acting, this may bring some hope to Harrisburg schools.

A key then will be how that money is spent. Among things needed are improved counseling, nursing, and varied extra-curricular activities for students. Doing this will help address the social problems that face Harrisburg students. Students can learn to rise above their problems. We need teachers, administrators, and counselors who may direct students towards achieving these successes.

****

The Way Votes Are Gotten: Let's Get Back to Our Grassroots

November 3, 2014

Today is election day.

For the first time in my life, I have never received a single mailed political advertisement for this election. I have not received a single phone call regarding this election, not even from one of those robots who call. I have not had a single party committee person or campaign volunteer ask for my vote.

I am reminded how the late U.S. House Speaker Tip O'Neill entitled his autobiography "All Politics is Local." O'Neill came to that realization when he was running for Congress. After he saw someone he knew had voted, he expressed his presumption that she had just voted for him. She told him she had not voted for him. Stunned, he asked why she has not voted for him. She told him she did not vote for him because he never asked for her vote.

Politics used to involve human interaction. As much as I have criticized "machine politics" over the years, there was a low cost effective simplicity to it. Your local committee people of both parties would see you received written information about the candidates. They would speak with you and answer questions. You would go vote at the polls and your committee people would be there to greet you and answer any more questions (keeping the proper distance away from the polling entrance). Over time, if the committee people are good, you learn to trust them and their perspectives. The committee people would keep tabs on who has voted, and towards the end of the day they would have people run out and remind people who hadn't voted what times the polls close.

Several studies indicate that effective committee people might improve the vote totals for their candidates by perhaps five to ten percentage points over the vote totals in similar areas where there were not effective committee people. While it seems like a lot of work to get just a handful of extra votes, those percentages are often the difference between defeat and victory.

While it involved a lot of work, the key to all this is is it did not involve a lot of money. This was low cost grass roots politics at its best.

If Tip O'Neill were to write his autobiography today, it might be titled "No Politics is Local." There are some remnants of the human interaction type of politics, yet that is becoming rarer.

I once address a local political organization about the committee people system and their response was mostly, "it sounds like too much work." I was then loudly lambasted by a state party official who told how politics now depends all on media, fund raising, and that what I had suggested was a waste of time.

That state party official correctly identified what politics has since become. Politics is virtually all media advertising. The vast majority of commercials (as verified by the Annenberg School of Communications) are negative ads. So basically, politics has become us watching the television and learning how bad the candidates are.

The Citizens United decision by the U.S Supreme Court has vastly increased campaign advertising. The ruling that there can be no limits on how much one spends on a political campaign or issue has allowed those with wealth and access to wealth to dominate the media with campaign advertising. Again, much of it is negative advertising telling us what is wrong with a candidate.

If the press is trying to figure out why voter turn out is low, I present my views above. People are not given as many reasons as to why they should vote for candidates. Further, at least in my part of Harrisburg, no one has not asked us to vote for them. I have not had a knock at my door. I have not seen a representative of any candidate nor received a single piece of campaign literature. Of course, there have been an avalanche of television ads.

We need laws restraining and hopefully eventually overturning the damages Citizens United has done. We need to tell candidates to give us more reasons why we should vote for them rather than telling us why we should not vote for their opponents. It might even help that grass roots politics returns. While it will take time, I do believe some future Harrisburg political leader will figure that out.

****

Solving Intellectual Disability and Drug / Alcohol Dependency Problems

November 22, 2014

What should we do with Harrisburg Hospital?

In looking back, it may have been a long term mistake to have closed it. While it serves as a symbol of failed intellectual disability (i.e. as mental health) programs, as highlighted by its depiction in the movie "Girl, Interrupted", we have since made great improvements in intellectual disability treatments. We now know more about intellectual disabilities and how to more properly treat them. We also have developed more effective treatments and we have also improved awareness of how to better counsel people with intellectual disabilities.

We need more mental health and intellectual disability facilities.

We need to apply the common sense wisdom of the past, which was hampered by a lack of knowledge, with the knowledge we have gained although we have lost the common sense wisdom.

The common sense wisdom is when someone has a problem, we should try to solve that individual's problem. The lack of common sense is the notion that everyone's problems should be dealt with in the same manner (i.e. "throw them in prison and throw away the key"). We are now in that era where common sense is lacking.

There are, and have been, people who were unable to conform to societal norms to such a degree that the Commonwealth of Pennsylvania places them into a state institution. A few decades ago, about 90% of people institutionalized were placed into an intellectual disability facility. About 10% of those placed in a state institution were placed into state prison. This is how things were when George Leader was Governor. I credit George Leader for pointing this fact out to me.

Several decades ago, many people in mental health and intellectual disability facilities were badly treated. They were abused and or neglected. These facilities, correctly, were closed. Many patients were released into society. Freed, many had difficulties adjusting to society, found poor housing from landlords who ripped them off, experienced high rates of sexual and physical abuse, wound up using drugs and/or alcohol, became homeless, and were incarcerated.

Since then, great advances have occurred in counseling, psychology, and psychiatry, There is a greater understanding of various problems and how to better treat them. Great strides have been made in knowing how to provide better treatment for drug and/or alcohol dependencies. Yet we have generally not applied these advances in services to those who need them.

Today, about 90% of people institutionalized by the Commonwealth are in prison and about 10% are in mental health and intellectual disability treatment. This is a tremendous turnover from just a few decades ago when those percentages were reversed.

We as a society have decided to take away counseling for those with difficulties. We instead have decided to both imprison more people and to keep them in prison for much longer terms. Prisons have sparse and inadequate counseling services, When released from prison, a person likely still has the same intellectual disability behavior that brought that person to prison. That difficulty has usually not been adequately addressed. Indeed, prisoners often are released from spending time with other criminals having learned how to become better criminals.

As we've improved how to treat troubled people, we have deliberately chosen instead not to provide help to people in overcoming their problems. We instead have moved towards the more expensive alternative, which is increasing incarceration. Providing counseling is the least expensive, by far, means of dealing with these problems. The sooner problems are identified, such as when a troubled person is still in school, the more likely the problems can be resolved and the person may go on to lead a more productive life with fewer difficulties.

Incarceration is the most expensive method. It has been one of the fastest growing costs in state budgets as few in the public have questioned these huge costs as we keep electing "anti-crime" elected official. (As if their opponents were "pro-crime", yet that is a separate discussion on distorted election perceptions and creating fear among voters in order to win votes. There is also a separate discussion to be had on the politics of campaign contributions and awarding contracts constructing prisons and in operating justice facilities. The "kids for cash" scandal where judges received kickbacks for ordering children to private juvenile justice facilities is a prime example.).

It is indeed ironic, on the other hand, that while voters often claim that education is a priority to them, we have turned our backs on valuable school counseling programs. In this era of tightened school budgets, funds have been severely cut for counselors and health care professionals who should have been serving those children with problems. Children with developmental problems that are not resolved often fall behind academically, fail to fit in with their peers and become more socially awkward as adults. These often are the adults who may find themselves with crime as a career choice and drug alcohol dependency as a life choice.

I recall speaking with an official at Columbine High School years ago following shootings there where several died. He spoke at a conference where it appeared nearly all attending agreed that more early intervention school counseling programs could prevent further similar tragedies. Most teachers, school nurses, and school psychologists can identify around fifth grade which students are having problems adjusting. This does not mean each such student will become a murderer. Yet by providing appropriate counseling and treatment, these troubled students can learn to adjust, improve their grades, and have better futures.

With each successive tragedy, I see scholars, academicians, and others getting together and each time they arrive at similar conclusions. We need to get more children into counseling and treatment programs earlier in life.

While the needs are known, little is being done to achieve what needs to be done. It is time we finally stop talking about obvious solutions and create these solutions. Unfortunately, there is no mass movement of people with mental health problems, intellectual difficulties, and dependencies organizing to obtain support of programs supporting them. We need to advocate for those who cannot help themselves or do not yet know they will need these services. We need to speak for those who can not speak for themselves. We do not need more tragedies where we agree something needs to be done, then forget about it until there are more tragedies, thus repeating this fruitless cycle. We need to act in the interests of people with current and future needs as well as in our own interests as long term taxpayers and as potential victims of people with problems.

When people realize that so many lives will improve and that money will be saved, hopefully there will be an outpouring of support and action.

Footnote: There are career criminals who are a separate category from the above discussion. Some Criminologists believe that about one half of one percent of prisoners are career criminals who have made a decision to engage in and remain criminals.

Some Psychologists have found some success with empathy treatment to get criminals to learn to identify with their victims and understand the hurt they cause.

****

How Harrisburg Can Solve Disputes

December 19, 2014

Conflict happens between all kinds of people and groups. Conflicts happen between neighbors and street gangs. Conflicts happen between officials and governments. It is important that such conflicts are resolved by productive talks and not with fighting, division, or warfare.

The late Muzafer Sharif, who taught Psychology at Penn State, was among those who used to show people locally and elsewhere how to resolve conflicts. His techniques are still used in public administration studies on resolving political conflicts. While they were presented for political or business negotiations, Sharif hoped that they could someday be used towards achieving world peace.

In Harrisburg, we can use what he taught to find resolutions with many local disagreements that currently exist.

A key in negotiations is to discover what the common interests of the involved individuals and groups are. Areas of disagreement are to be avoided during discussions, and areas of commonality are to be emphasized.

Many discussions or relationships break-up over upsetting words. The idea is to shift the focus to how parties may mutually work to improve each others' interests. When parties find ways to work together, conceivably they will discover ways to resolve their differences or at least realize their mutual goals are more more important than their differences.

For instance, conflict resolution between street gangs gets them to realize how similar they are. Gang members are typically similar age people who are seeking bonds with others their age. Instead of fighting each other, they should be seeking ways to connect with one other. If they can not bond together, they should at least respect the rights of other groups to exist. When they realize they are hurting others and getting hurt themselves over the temporary concept of "turf", the need for hurting each other should disappear.

The work of Sharif emerged from his research demonstrating how these principles operate. Sharif asked people in a dark room to look at a candlelight. He then asked people to write down which direction the light moved. People saw the movement with their own eyes. They would be surprised at any mention that the light had moved in the opposite direction. How can one disagree with something that one had seen with one's own eyes?

Those who saw the movement in a particular direction were placed together and introduced to a group of people who argued the candle had moved in another direction. To each group, it often was an abhorrent idea that someone would dare challenge what people knew from personal observation to be correct. Thus, they often concluded that anyone who dared to refuse to admit to what is known truth has to be unstable, unobservant, dangerous, etc. The fact that they were being confronted with others who steadfastly insisted on their version of what happened and who refused to compromise only further tended to create further aggravation.

It mattered a lot how the discussions went. If the two groups could agree that people are free to hold and respect their own views, discussions often concluded without much drama, and the parties became friendly.

However, if discussions contained hurtful words or insults, the harmed party would often take deep offense. This often solidified the position of those who believed their views to be correct and made them feel as if the other side was both a denier of reality and harmful to their own beliefs. This made them angrier. Their anger often made the other side angrier. If one side believes an attack is coming its way—either verbally in discussions or physically in wars or fights—a preemptive strike may be contemplated.

The disagreements can quickly escalate into wider differences. As a result, such negotiations often failed to make the groups friendly and usually made them more bitter enemies.

The truth is the candlelight never moved. By staring at a candlelight in a dark room, the mind plays tricks and makes people think the light moved. In fact, it was still the entire time.

If people are brought together in the same dark room and discussions are cordial, people will begin seeing the candlelight move in the same direction when a moderator or leader states the candlelight is moving in a particular direction. The mind is susceptible to suggestions. If people start angrily arguing about which direction the candlelight is moving, others will also have differing perceptions of how the candlelight moves. This tends to enhance the disagreements. A movement towards mutual visualization of how the candlelight moves occurs when people finally verbally agree upon the movements.

Of course, learning the truth that the candlelight never moved should let everyone understand that they all had the same experiences and that there was never any need to argue.

Sharif saw this as a useful study not only of the mind's psychology but also on the interactions of human behavior. He saw this as a means towards getting people to relate better with each other. Sharif saw this as a means towards achieving peaceful settlements of disputes.

The Sharif studies are a useful analogy for conflicts from local ones like in Harrisburg to international disputes. One group often has its own perceptions and the members of the group may be intolerant of those whose perceptions differ from theirs. When they communicate and focus on matters which the parties involved agree, they can increase the amount of matters upon which they can find mutual agreements. They hopefully will become friends rather than enemies. Ultimately and ideally, world peace can be achieved.

And if that's true, then it indicates peace in Harrisburg can be achieved.

Note: Naysayers on resolving gang conflicts argue many gangs are involved in criminal activities and that the means to deal with them is to put them in prison. This is a discussion of a separate issue of reducing violence within a community. Criminal activity is to be properly determined by police and the judicial system. Negotiators have a different mission of resolving conflicts.

****

YWCA of Greater Harrisburg Confronts Human Trafficking

January 30, 2015 ·

If a tree falls in the forest when no human is around, does it make a sound?

Of course the falling of a tree onto the ground makes a sound. Plus, for the tree, falling

down is a life changing moment. Not only that, but there are

numerous subsequent effects on the surrounding environment from the fallen tree.

There is a related question. If there is a noise yet no concerned human responds, does

the situation matter?

Let me alternatively ask this question: If a person who has been humanly trafficked

stands in front of you, will be able to tell that person has been sold in modern slavery?

The YWCA of Greater Harrisburg has received a grant to study human tracking. This is

a great news. Opening awareness so we hear there is a problem is a key step forward.

We are finally hearing the noises of fallen lives.

I am not an expert in human trafficking. I have discussed the issues with some experts.

It is their belief that human trafficking exists far more extensively than we care to admit.

It is easier to cast our eyes away. The experts believe human trafficking victims are here, standing in front of us, right here in Harrisburg and across the world.

Police experts generally will state they lack the resources to do much about human trafficking. We place a low priority on this type of crime and dispute these crimes' viciousness. We care more about the crimes we see and report. It is far more difficult to investigate and report hidden crimes where few report them.

We often only learn about the crimes when something goes wrong, such as when a boat filled with people being brought into the nation illegally is seized or is found during an emergency rescue.

Few of those brought into this country report the crime. To some, they are escaping a worse life of greater poverty. Some have saved and paid someone to bring them to the United States. They then work in illegal industries, from factories with no windows for outsiders to see in to work in the sex industry. Some may hide in plain sight in various retail and agricultural positions as they are scurried about to avoid developing community attachments.

Great Britain and Ireland are taking initial measures. What is being found is horrific. For those who abhor slavery, literal slave trade continues with bidders ranging from factory owners to massage parlor chains who bid on workers. The "bought people's" passports are taken away and their lives illegally belong to those who purchase them. A British study notes their police are attempting to break through, discover, and stop human traffickers. Some believe crack downs on human trafficking in other countries are driving more human trafficking business to the United States.

We are not as proactive in stopping this.

Many people trafficked into the United States are unaware they have rights. We need labor rights brochures (including how to safely report violations) to be written and posted around areas where we suspect there could be illegal employment. These brochures should be written in many languages, particularly those languages from which it is believed people are being trafficked. They should be posed (and reposted as they will be torn down) and distributed in areas where illegal operations may occur and where immigrant populations live. Such places could be truck stops, grocery stores, and convenience stores.

Not all human trafficking is of foreigners. There are domestic victims, often people with limited work and housing options whose situation is exploited by illegal employers. Similarly, such people may find themselves in illegal industrial, agriculture, or sex work.

A major problem is we treat the victims as criminals. If their place of work is raided, the trafficked employees are arrested. They may be imprisoned or deported. Often the managers know how to escape. The investigations seldom reach up and arrest the traffickers.

The lucrative business of human trafficking continues because it is difficult to stop. We need to commit or shift more resources towards stopping it. We also need to start treating the victims as victims and assisting them, advising them of their rights, and helping them get out of illegal activities and learn how to enter legal employment.

We need to stop being blind to this. It is happening. It impacts many lives.

The YWCA of Greater Harrisburg is taking needed steps. There are many victims out there, and we need to reach out and help them.

****

How the City of Harrisburg and Others Should Manage Their Money

February 22, 2015

When I attended the Wharton School, I had a concentration in Finance.

This was a tough concentration to obtain. Half the students who took Finance 1 failed. Half the students who took Finance 2 failed. Those who passed both and went into the higher level courses learned the deep, dark secret of Finance. I am now going to share the secret of Finance with you and hope that our Harrisburg city government investors and Pennsylvania state investors are reading and taking notes, too.

Take the listing of all the companies issuing stock found in newspapers such as the Wall Street Journal (for young people who have trouble understanding what a newspaper is, don't worry….you can print out of the listing of companies you can find on the WSJ website). Take these pages and tape them somewhere you don't mind getting holes in the wall (i.e. use a friend's basement). Obtain 30 darts. Blindfold yourself or someone else (no, this has nothing to do with 50 shades of anything). Point the blindfolded person in the direction of the list of companies offering stocks. Throw the 30 darts at the list, randomly hitting names of companies. Take your financial portfolio and invest it in shares of each of these 30 companies a dart hit.

Congratulations. If you do this, you are now most likely in the top fifth of financial advisors nationwide.

The reason why this works is that no one knows the future. Thus, any well diversified portfolio should have strong long term returns. It takes about 30 stocks to develop a well diversified portfolio. I recall lectures by Lawrence Klein who developed econometrics which shows how current economic events can more likely result in future economic events. Yet even these predictions are made within margins of error and sometimes prove wrong. As for stock market prices, these prices are quickly and efficiently determined within minutes on stock exchange floors. Most financial managers engage in research speculation at best and often are just guessing. A book that has remerged on the best seller list, "A Random Walk Down Wall Street" by Burton Malkiel explains in depth how no financial analyst has developed a mathematical pattern that can accurately predict future stock market prices (See Footnote for one unimportant exception to this.).

The reason why randomly picking 30 stocks and holding onto them will make you among the best performers in stock market returns is simple. Money is lost on transition and administrative costs. If you pick and buy your own stocks and hold onto them, you do not pay all these costs. It is those who "wheel and deal" with their brokers who often fare poorly because their investments are eaten away by broker costs.

The key to lowering broker costs is to use brokers as little as possible. Governments, including the City of Harrisburg, should keep this in mind. The city will likely fare much better having a few skilled professional financial advisors on the payroll than to turn the management of their funds to outside brokerage firms.

One would especially be foolish to have thirty-seven brokers. If you had thirty-seven brokers, you should be on some TV reality show for hoarding brokers. That is just too many to have.

That being said, it seems the Pennsylvania Treasury has thirty-seven brokers. When I read that the State Treasurer's office uses thirty-seven brokerage firms and that managers from most of these firms made campaign contributions to candidates for the State Treasurer's office, I thought to myself, "Well, that is a problem waiting to happen." Oops, I guess that did happen. This may explain why Rob McCord is now a former State Treasurer.

As an aside, I also do not believe that administrative offices that manage more than establish public policies should be elected positions. Offices such as State Treasurer, Auditor General, Attorney General, City Treasurer (another office that has seen a few messes), Prothonotary, Recorder of Deeds, etc. do not need to be elected. These are administrative positions that could be appointed. A person appointed to a position is more likely to have better qualifications than would an elected politician. Electing such offices invites those seeking to benefit from their office operations to seek to obtain that influence through campaign donations. Granted, making these positions appointed rather than elected will not remove all politics from these positions. Yet, it will prevent interest groups making improper inroads with political donations.

So, to the city government and to others, save money by not giving it to wealthy brokerage firms. How do you think they became wealthy big firms in the first place?

Footnote: There are a few people who know I am aware of an exception to the above article. I am aware of someone who developed a model that might have put him towards the top of financial managers. I successfully determined what he was doing. It is of questionable legality and definitely immoral, yet, when did that ever stop a stock broker?

Also, for complete honestly, my Finance Professor used tarot cards rather than darts. The concept is the same. I just understand darts better than tarot cards.

****

Here's a Plan for City Planning

February 28, 2015

There is a very easy way to handle city planning in Harrisburg. The way to resolve city planning is this: ask the people living there what they want.

The history of urban development, zoning, and city planning has been often been that some centralized powers and developers decide what they believe is best for a city, and then they impose what they believe is right onto communities. Oh, sure they do formally seek public comment from a public that is generally unaware something is about to happen until it occurs.

Decades ago, entire communities were torn down in the City of Harrisburg to make way for government buildings and various projects. People lament the disappearance of the Old 8th Ward, a poor but vibrant community. A horrendous result was that displaced residents were promised new homes. Only a handful of people were actually relocated to residences in Allison Hill.

No one asked these residents if they wanted their homes torn down and be forced to scatter to find what low income housing they could. I suspect most would have been against this. Even when building and house removals are essential for the greater public services, the residents should have had more say in their destinies.

There is often a lot of history and great architecture in homes slated for demolishment. What often is ignored by planners and developers is that residents have formed bonds and a community spirit. Those deserve strong consideration in determining a community's destination,

Harrisburg is already close to offering what a large number of people seek. Many people want a community where one may safely travel and obtain what they need in groceries, exercise, entertainment, etc. within walking distance. There are advantages to this mixed use zoning both in improving lives and in decreasing reliance on automobiles and gas.

Residents should be asked what they want. Perhaps they want the city to act quickly and remove a blighted house. If the property can't be sold for new home construction, perhaps it can become a community park, or perhaps it can become a community garden. Urban gardening is gaining strength as residents find it both good exercise and a means to keep the costs of food reduced.

(As an aside, some Harrisburg homes, especially those with flat roofs, could make good locations for rooftop urban gardens. This both provides low cost food and can help lower that house's energy costs.)

There is talk of a comprehensive plan being developed. Then in order to make the process as publicly inclusive as possible, Harrisburg should create volunteer neighborhood planning groups. These groups should meet, hold public hearings, and pass along the recommendations of local residents to the Mayor, City Council, the Planning Commission, and the Zoning Board. Most important, the volunteers should go around and ask what people want. Public desires and ideas need to be heard, considered, and acted upon.

****

Cancer Awareness

Bonus Column

October is Breast Cancer Awareness Month. It is good for everyone to be checked for all kinds of cancer. Cancer is often preventable and curable. Being examined for cancer can lead to longer and healthier lives.

Harrisburg residents have their own particularly good reason for taking extra precautions. We have, compared to most others, increased exposure to radiation.

I am not out to create a panic. These higher levels of radiation exposure have been going on for decades now. Most of us seem to not be noticeably affected by this. I know there are readers out there who will be quick to point out there do not seem to be any statistically significant increased rates of most cancers in Harrisburg.

I even observed one politician claim that radiation is good for you. I suspect this politician found those paint chips he ate as a child were delicious.

There is much debate in the scientific community as to what actually causes cancer. There are numerous things that have been proven to increase cancers. Harrisburg is full of them: water traveling through lead pipes, people eating yummy burned red meat on our many restaurants, smoking those addictive cigarettes found in a few stores, drinking tasty chemicals in diet soda, etc.

Everyone is different. Some people have brief exposures to carcinogens and develop cancer. Others work and live in conditions surrounded by carcinogens and never develop cancers. Developing cancer could involved exposure to several different risks rather than just one. Genetics can be a factor. (Link to American Cancer Society at cancer.org for more information.)

There is one particular potential cancer source that is fairly unique to Harrisburg. Perhaps you have heard of it. It is called Three Mile Island. If you are not familiar with it, you may be alone from a lot of the rest of the world. When traveling to foreign countries, an oft heard response when declaring one is from Harrisburg is "You're from Three Mile

Island!" Some foreigners appear disappointed that we do not, as rumored, glow in the dark.

If you seriously have not heard of it, I recommend you look up "Three Mile Island" in your favorite search engine and read about this bit of local history. It helped publicize a Jane Fonda movie.

For several decades now, radiation trapped in Three Mile Island nuclear plant has been deliberately slowly leaked out to alleviate adverse pressure. This is well known. It was joked decades ago that today people in Harrisburg would become mutants. We would all look grotesque. Sadly, our careers in zombie movies never materialized. Other than a few photographs of Harrisburg residenst taken after over consumption on Second Street bars, a quick visual survey of our residents confirms most of us look alright.

Most of us have become either accepting or ignorant of any health threats from nuclear energy radiation leakages. After all, the President of the United States went inside Three Mile Island and declared it safe.

I always liked the progression in those proclamations that Three Mile Island was safe. They sent the Lieutenant Governor in first to proclaim it was safe. After the Lieutenant Governor appeared alright, they sent the Governor in to proclaim it was safe. After the Governor seemed alright, then the President went inside Three Mile Island.

An interesting irony is that it was not always felt that nuclear power was so safe. In fact, just before Three Mile Island, there was growing evidence from the University of Pittsburgh and elsewhere that it was not safe. The interesting result of Three Mile Island being unsafe is it seems to have created the forces that quashed the very studies that may have shown it was not safe.

Ernest Sterglass, a University of Pittsburgh Professor who led their Radiation and Public Health Project, was finding data, just prior to the Three Mile Island incident, that cancer rates may be affected by radiation leakages occurring at other nuclear power plants. The cancer rates increased the closer people were living near the nuclear power plants. There was a strong hypothesis that the spikes in cancer rates were attributable to the nuclear power plants' radiation leakages. (Link to "Secret Fallout" by Ernest Sternglass, available for free download at ratical.org/radiation/SecretFallout/).

These studies were preceded by ones conducted by Alice Stewart, who headed Oxford University's Social and Preventive Medicine Department. She had discovered health risks to children exposed to low levels of radiation. She then studied nuclear power radiation risks with Thomas Mancuso of the University of Pittsburgh. Sternglass followed with his own research.

After Three Mile Island, there emerged an effort to reassure the public that nuclear radiation is safe. I recall speaking with Environmental Protection Agency employees who spoke about the changes in attitude. A new President Ronald Reagan was supportive of nuclear power. Reagan was elected defeating Jimmy Carter, a nuclear engineer, and John Anderson, who sponsored the Price-Anderson Act that limited the liability of nuclear power companies for losses from any nuclear accidents. The new attitude among many public officials was to declare nuclear energy as safe to our heath. The result of Three Mile Island was not massive public objections to nuclear power. The result was general public acceptance of nuclear power.

Funding for research showing the problems of nuclear energy began disappearing. Industry researchers began questioning the past data. They used different radiation levels to show different results. They conducted different analyses. The U.S. Nuclear Regulatory Commission claims there were "no detectable" health consequences from the Three Mile Island incidence. Or, at least none they could find. (Link to: U.S. Nuclear Regulatory Commission, "Backgrounder on the Three Mile Island Accident" at nrc.gov/reading-rm/doc-collections/fact-sheets/3mile-isle.html)

When local residents, suspicious of local cancer rate increases, attempted to take the issue to court, it was the court findings that the cancer rates for the metropolitan area showed no increases. A Pennsylvania Health Department Select Committee found that months after the Three Mile Island crisis the rates of hypothyroidism increased twelve times above normal downwind where the leakages traveled. (Link to: Gordon K. MacLeod, "A Role for Public Health", American Journal of Public Health, March 1982, at aphapublications.org/doi/pdf/10.2105/AJPH.72.3.237) Yet, considering the entire area and not just those fewer "downwind", our court system determined these rates were inconsequential.

I am not a radiation researcher. I would expect that using a larger population data drowned out any localized cancer rate increases. The courts, in their wisdom (or lack thereof) made a legal conclusion there were no health risks from the radiation leakages

.

The U.S. Labor Department reached a different conclusion. They concluded that employees at nuclear weapons facilities, due to their work, have higher risks for cancer than do people who worked elsewhere. There will be readers who will argue these facilities were different. That is the point. These were not facilities leaking as much radiation as does Three Mile Island. The Labor Department has paid over $65 million compensation to over 1,000 employees. (Link to Hartford Business Journal at hartfordbusiness,com/article/201406109992 and to the Division of Energy Employees Occupational Compensation at dol.gov/owcp/energy/))

A legal determination is not a scientific one. Some studies that hypothesized there are health concerns from radiation leakages were not allowed to be completed. This research should be revitalized. We must let proper research determine the health risks, if any, from the radiation leaking from power plants.

Studies need to realize that the population to be studied is mobile. I recall listening to a number of women were were 17 years old when the Three Mile Island crisis happened. They all lived near Three Mile Island. They returned for a reunion, many living in various places around the country. It seemed quite coincidental that several mentioned they were sterile and that physicians could not find a reason why that was.

No scientific conclusion can be drawn from that. I do recall some area veterinarians commenting that, after the Three Mile Island crisis, there appeared to have been an increase in still births and infertility among cattle and other mammals. Humans are mammals. Few studied the effects on animals after Three Mile Island beyond testing milk, so I admit this is all conjecture. Proper scientific studies should determine if these serious concerns are real.

If studies do reemerge that look at health risks of those exposed to radiation leakages, we must consider some data challenges. Looking at the cancer rates of people currently living in the Harrisburg area muddles the figures. Many of those who were here when the Three Mile Island incident have moved away. Many people have moved in since. Area residents have had different years and levels of exposures to the subsequent radiation leakages. This needs to be taken into account.

So, to be safe, just in case the old hypotheses are correct: Watch out for signs of cancer. See a physician regularly. Harrisburg residents may or may not be at higher risks for some kinds of cancer. So protect yourselves.

****

Agricultural Safety

Bonus Column

There is a spread of Pork Epidemic Diarrhea Virus (PEDv) around central Pennsylvania. Yes, it as gross as it sounds. It kills young pigs. It is found in older pigs and sickens them yet they survive. To be fair to the pork industry, they reassure us the pigs with PEDv virus are safe to eat.

Credit goes to Harrisburg's own Bill Keisling and his Yardbird publications for discovering this outbreak. This is an excellent example of the use of investigative journalism. We need more people who examine and question what is happening.

PEDv disease reached the United States last year. It has now reached our local farms. This is something relatively new that we must learn how to handle,

Meats should be thoroughly cooked, regardless. All meat can contain contaminants. Nearly all raw chickens sold contain harmful substances.

This PEDv event raises critical policy issues. First, as Yardbird points out, the state Agriculture Department states there is nothing they can be do about this problem.

The Agriculture Department is unable to act to intercede in a virus that can cause significant economic loss to local farmers.

The matter goes far beyond the PEDv crisis. The Agriculture Department can not react to most any crisis. They react to problems brought to their attention. Then they analyze the data and seek conclusions to what diseases may exist.

The Agriculture Department does not have the legal authority to be proactive. This solution should be obvious. The legislature and Governor should allow this. Industry may object, yet industry needs to be saved from itself. The health and safety of consumers and products needs to come first.

The Agriculture Department needs more resources. They can test for a limited number of health threats. As more goods come in from other countries, they need to be able to test for a wider range of potential threats, many of which may be new to Pennsylvania.

There are many health threats worldwide that are beyond the Agriculture Department's abilities to identify.

The limiting of state government to being reactive rather than proactive is not limited to the Agriculture Department. The same problem is found with the Health Department.

A seemingly lax approach to health dangers is not the fault of Health Department employees. It is our fault for not demanding the legislature and the Governor to insist that both the Health and Agriculture Departments proactively seek to identify health concerns, warn others, help those affected, and take actions to prevent the illness from spreading.

There are been instances when people, pets, and farm products have become diseased and died. It is up to someone to report this to the Agriculture Department. If they feel it is appropriate, they will conduct tests and see if there is something happening that can be spread.

The Health Department has excellent records of health data. Yet they just basically publish the data. They don't issue commentary. It is up to someone else to do the research and determine if there are reasons why there may be clusters of health concerns.

Some clusters are just statistical flukes. Some are chance happenings that a large number of people contaminated each other.

Many health clusters indicate a problem exists. Sometimes a disease outbreak may have an environmental cause.

In Pennsylvania, it happens that an industrial spill or leakages from an old mine or contaminated worksite can sickened people. One would need to have knowledge of both these environmental facts and health information to put these together.

The Health, Agriculture, and Environmental Protection Departments have no legal mandate to examine each others' data to determine if they may find connections. This is something the legislature and Governor should legally require.

It is often up to the public to find suspicious patterns and question them. Yet few people have the expertise to do this. There have been past successes found by investigative journalists.

It has been reporters, familiar with local spills, leaks, and other hazards who have found connections between environmental hazards and increased health concerns. It often took newspapers that made commitments to investigative reporters to discover these facts.

The sad thing is newspapers are dying, with many already dead. Those that survive are cutting back staff. Investigative reporters are often among those staff that are cut.

We now are in an era where the Internet produces more people able to express their views on public forums. At the same time, it is reducing the ability of news organizations to hire expert reporters who can take a long period of time to research a complicated issue.

That is why I note is was an investigative reporter Bill Keisling who broke the story about the PEDv. We need more, not fewer, such writers.

We also need government to require itself to act as its own investigative researchers. We need to have people with legal authority to research and act on health and public safety matters.

We should demand that our government actively protect us.

We also need a free and active press to protect us from government inaction and wrongful government action.

****

Substance Abuse

Bonus column

Leon Czikowsky discontinued his column when he was hired by government to work on policy issues. The following column combines two he wrote while working. His superiors requested any column he wrote receive their approvals before he published them. The columns were neither accepted nor rejected for publication. They were kept on hold for several months. Since Leon Czikowsky has left government employment, they are now published as one column. These were not submitted to "Today's the Day Harrisburg" nor were edited or seen by anyone at "Today's the Day Harrisburg".

A misreading of a journal publication has led to the greatest cause of death of middle age white males.

The leading cause of death of Caucasian males, aged 45 to 54, is drug overdose. Since 2000, it has surpassed diabetes, chronic liver diseases, suicides, and then lung cancer to become what most kills middle aged white men. What makes this statistic even more frightening is that substance abuse is also associated with most of the chronic liver diseases and many of the suicide deaths. Added together, drugs are directly and indirectly, by far, the leading reason why a middle age white male dies.

This is strictly an American phenomenon. The death rates for middle aged white males has decreased in other countries, contrary to what is happening here. The reason is because we Americans consume far more prescription pharmaceutical drugs than do people outside America.

It is not just middle age white males dying from drug overdoses. It is just that this statistic sticks out. Any preconception that it is just "druggies" who are overdosing is wrong. It is estimated that 6.5 million Americans abused Oxycontin, a legally prescribed pharmaceutical, compared to there being 500,000 Americans using crack cocaine. It is estimated that one in four families have at least one member suffering from substance abuse. Substance abuse occurs amongst every demographic type of American.

One of the reasons why substance abuse affects every type of American is prescription drugs are over prescribed. This is making many people addicted or dependent upon these drugs. From high school students with bodily injuries to middle age people with back aches to older citizens with creaking joints, physicians have prescribed powerful drugs to handle pain. What many physicians do not realize is that these drugs are addictive.

The reason many physicians do not realize this is because they were told the drugs would not be addictive. This is where the misreading of a journal publication becomes critical. OxyContin was marketed to physician as an essentially non-addictive drug. It was claimed that only 1% of its users would become addicted. Physicians had no reason to doubt this and thus freely dispensed OxyContin and other pain relievers.

Physicians in fact were pressured to dispense pain relievers. During the early 1990s and before, physicians did not prescribe narcotics for pain. In 1992, there were organizations, heavily associated with pharmaceutical manufacturers, which began declaring there is a need for pain management. Physicians who refused to do this were ridiculed for allowing their patients to remain in pain. The concerns of Medical Associations that the pain medications could be addictive was handled by their successfully lobbying state legislatures to make physicians immune from liability should patients become addictive. Treating pain with narcotics has become standard practice.

Why would physicians knowingly prescribe medications even when they correctly feared were addictive? They did so because the drug manufacturers assured them that the drugs were safe. It turns out the basis for these claims was from misrepresenting a journal publication.

In 1980, the New England Journal of Medicine published a letter from a physician stating that, of 12,000 hospitalized under physician care, when given low doses of opiates, resulted in a one per cent addiction rate.

This letter was misinterpreted as a journal article (not a letter) stating that the use of larger doses of opiates (not low doses, as the letter stated) given to patients to take home (not in physician controlled hospitalization settings as the letter stated) would result in a one percent addiction rate (which still indicates a need to monitor for addiction being a result). It seems few, if anyone, checked if this was correct, in part because this journal was archived online only back to their 1993 issues.

The Federal government prosecuted the drug manufacturer that made this misleading claim. The case was settled for a $634.5 million fine. Still, the company continues selling OxyContin with annual sales over $3 billion annually.

As Oxycontin and other opioids continue being sold, people are dying from using them. It is not just white middle age men but people of all kinds who are taking opioids for pain and dying from opiate overdoses. Some opioid users turn to heroin, another opiate which, while illegal, is actually often less expensive than legal opioids.

Opioid overdoses are rapidly increasing and have become a major cause of death for all age groups of both sexes. We need to act to handle this problem. We need to expand the number of drug treatment facilities. We need to convince more people abusing opioids to get treatment. We need to make more opioid abusers aware that treatment exists and is possible.

This leading health care crisis is solvable. It requires actions. We need now to do that which is necessary to save many lives.

Former Governor George Leader stated one of the most important lessons he wanted people to realize was, when he was Governor, which was a few years after I was born, 90% of the people institutionalized by the Commonwealth were in public health treatment and 10% were imprisoned. Today, 90% of the people institutionalized by the Commonwealth are imprisoned and 10% are in public health treatment.

During our lifetimes, we effectively made a public policy choice that we would take the vast majority of people experiencing health and social problems and, instead of providing treatment so they may overcome their difficulties, we throw them into prisons and jails. We did this incrementally without debating what we did. It is time we open these discussions.

Statistics prove this is exactly what we have done. Data shows that 70% to 80% of people who are incarcerated are so a result of substance abuse. They were either selling or possessing illegal drugs, committed an offense to afford to purchase illegal substances, or they committed the crime while under the influence of an intoxicant.

Most of the people imprisoned for substance abuse are in their twenties. People at that age tend to do immature things. They usually become more mature, have jobs, form families, etc. in their thirties and beyond. Many people arrested in their twenties are given long prison sentences. In prison, they learn to become better criminals. While they are in prison, their children grow up without a parent. When they are released, the stigma of being a convict makes employment difficult. Long prison terms for substance abusers does not solve many problems and create many new ones.

Granted, some career criminals or people who committed horrific acts deserve to be incarcerated. The vast majority, though, are people like you, the reader, or someone you know, who took too many prescription pills or had a few too many drinks and become dependent or addicted to drugs and/or alcohol, who committed some offense and was caught. A Federal government survey indicated that one fifth of all Americans self-reported they had an addiction problem at some point in our life.

The most expensive method to handle people with these problems is to imprison them. It costs you, the taxpayer, billions of dollars every year keeping these people incarcerated. It costs tens of thousands of dollars per inmate every year. Effective treatment may cost only a few thousand dollars and in some drug free treatments even less.

It would be far less expensive to treat the substance abuse. Providing arrested people with an alternative of completing substance abuse treatment instead of being incarcerated or even proceeding to trial would save lots of money. More important, it would give many people healthier and more productive lives.

Substance abuse, in total, is the most costly health care cost. Estimates are that we provide treatment to approximately one tenth of substance abusers. There is no other major health care concern where we treat so few people.

We need to expand drug and alcohol treatment. We need to make substance abusers aware that treatment works, it is available, and we need to convince them to enter and complete treatment. This will take funding and outreach. The long term savings will be enormous. More important, many people will have improved lives.

Common sense states we should take our most expensive health care cost and treat it effectively. We instead treat substance abuse with the most expensive and least effective response, which is incarceration. It is time we use common sense and implement the correct treatment strategies towards solving our substance abuse crisis.

****

Sexual Abuse

Bonus column

The following column also was not submitted to "Today's the Day Harrisburg." It is written in response to a previous column.

Sigmund Freud, early in his career, made an important realization. We are a society of abusers. He presented a paper and learned a truth about society. A society of abusers does not want to be exposed. Anyone who attempts to expose this will be destroyed. Freud, wisely for his career, rewrote his paper, placing the blame on the victims rather than the abusers.

It has been widely claimed that one four women and one in six men are the victims of sexual assault. A study a few decades ago suggested these numbers may be low because people do not wish to admit this happened, even to themselves, and certainly not to surveys. This result suggested over one third of women were victims of sexual assault and concluded the rate for men is likely higher than one in six. A more recent survey found that one half of female college students---most of whom are in their late teens to early twenties---self-reported they had been victims of sexual assaults. This study noted that young people are more open and less likely to repress their past.

We as a society respond by focusing on the victims, which is appropriate. Victims need counseling and support. Psychology teaches about the Oedipus complex and how children exude sexuality. The results of this knowledge leads to a need for more counseling. Psychiatrists prescribe medications. Many people who can't afford psychiatrists self-medicate. Alcohol is the most commonly used self-medication, followed by pharmaceuticals, legal and illegal.Substance abuse, of legally prescribed and illegally obtained substances, has become so common it is now our nation's largest health care cost.

What we should also focus on is: Who are the abusers? I admit I don't know. There are people who have been arrested and incarcerated for abuse. That makes us feel good as a society that this problem has been at least partially addressed. It is often noted that many abusers have numerous victims. So the number of abusers should be less than the number of abused.

How many abusers are out there, undiscovered? We don't know. I believe we don't want to know. If so many people are being abused, then there have to be many abusers. The abusers do not want to be exposed. They do not want others to open the discussion to who abusers are. If so many people are being abused, whether it is one in six or one in two or over one in two over a lifetime, the answer is: There are many abusers, whatever the percent is.

Freud, Jung, and other psychologists have written, even if in brief references, that various hits and touches of children's erogenous zones are sexual. We need to look back at Freud's original observation, now suppressed. Why do we blame children, whose understanding of their actions are not well developed, for their seemingly sexual desires when it is the matured minded adult who did the touching? If the children can act in trauma later in life and respond by drowning their guilts with drugs and alcohol, it may be time we tell them their guilt is not their fault.

Some survey results find it is people in authority, be they relatives, institutional superiors, employers, etc. who commit the assaulting. People in power have the power to keep this discussion focused away from them.

It is time to focus the discussion on them.

I understand there will be resistance. For the record, I am an adult who has never abused a child. I was never abused as a child. I remember being in elementary and high school laughing at friends' jokes about these types of abuses. As humor is the brain realizing the irony of two incongruent thoughts, I found these jokes funny because I thought these events were incongruent. I did not think such abuse actually happened in the real world.

When I first researched and wrote about this topic, I realized how abusers respond. They claim that anyone looking into such topics must be an abuser, not them. Abusers threaten that such studies should stop---not much has changed since Freud's days--- and I did stop. Only now I realize who the real abusers are.

I am not a psychologist or childhood expert. I admit I am on only child, and both my parents were only children, and I never had children and my exposure to children is zilch. Yet I can read facts. I can observe.

What I see, and I will admit I could be wrong, is more openness and communication. This, in general, is good for most situations. It seems to me that most abusers were themselves abused. What they need is help, not incarceration. We can't afford, at least financially, to discover every abused and imprison them. What they need is counseling. They need to learn to overcome their guilt and to learn not to continue the cycle of abuse. They should learn that drugs and alcohol are not solutions and they create even more problems which often helps perpetuate the abuse.

We are a society need to recognize this problem that I fear is vast, but mostly hidden. We need to respond in a way that is also vast, yet one that will improve lives. We need to have more counselors, talk more to each other, allow others to be open in what they say to us, be more accepting of harsh truths that you hear, and have others be more accepting of harsh truths you have to say. The alternative is substance abuse, prison costs, and the continuation of abuse. That hasn't worked. If sanity is doing the same thing over and over and expecting a different result, I suggest the sane approach is to find another path to ending the insanity of abuse.

This page is intentionally left blank.

Except the print stating it has been intentionally left blank means the page is no longer blank.

The best of intentions are often not realized.

Yet we must strive to achieve the best results we can. That is how we improve ourselves.